Sales Forecasting

A Practical & Proven Guide to
Strategic Sales Forecasting

Gerard Assey

Sales Forecasting
A Practical & Proven Guide to Strategic Sales Forecasting

By
Gerard Assey

Published by:
Gerard Assey
19/18, Palli Arasan Street
Anna Nagar East
Chennai - 600 102

ISBN: 978-81-967202-6-1

(Image by jannoon028- courtesy Freepik: 'https://www.freepik.com' Thank You)

Table of Contents

- ✓ Preface
- ✓ Introduction to Sales Forecasting
- ✓ Importance of Forecasting in Business
- ✓ Why Accurate Forecasting is Crucial for Sales Managers
- ✓ Benefits of Reliable and Accurate Sales Forecasting
- ✓ Challenges in Accurate Sales Forecasting
- ✓ Key Points to Keep in Mind When Forecasting
- ✓ Methods and Techniques for Sales Forecasting
- ✓ How to Forecast Step by Step
- ✓ Validating the Forecast
- ✓ Strategic Opportunity Analysis and Forecast Management
- ✓ Identifying and Managing Forecast Killers
- ✓ Sales Forecasting Template
- ✓ Overcoming Key Forecasting Challenges
- ✓ Appendix: Templates and Tools for Practical Implementation
- ✓ Real-life Case Studies
- ✓ Interactive Exercises and Workshops
- ✓ Conclusion
- ✓ About the Author

Preface

Welcome to the world of "**Sales Forecasting: A Practical & Proven Guide to Strategic Sales Forecasting.**" In the dynamic landscape of business, accurate sales forecasting is not just a skill but a strategic imperative. As the heartbeat of organizational planning and decision-making, sales forecasting influences resource allocation, budgeting, and overall operational efficiency. This book is your comprehensive guide to navigating the intricate realms of sales forecasting, equipping you with the knowledge and tools to elevate your forecasting capabilities and contribute significantly to your organization's success.

The Journey Ahead

In the pages that follow, we embark on a journey that unfolds the intricacies of sales forecasting—from its historical evolution to cutting-edge techniques. Our goal is to demystify the process and empower you, whether you're a seasoned Sales Manager or a budding professional eager to grasp the essentials.

What You'll Find in this Book

Foundational Concepts: The book commences with an exploration of foundational concepts in sales forecasting. We define its scope, trace its historical evolution, and highlight its significance in modern business strategy. You'll gain a comprehensive understanding of the objectives and structure that will guide you through the chapters.

Importance and Benefits: Chapters dedicated to the importance of forecasting in business and the benefits of reliable predictions will illustrate how accurate forecasting is not just a managerial task but a linchpin for organizational success.

Managerial Perspective: Delve into the world of Sales Managers as we unveil why accurate forecasting is crucial for them. From setting realistic quotas to team motivation, we dissect the integral role that forecasting plays in a Sales Manager's myriad responsibilities.

Strategic Applications: Explore the strategic applications of accurate sales forecasting, from improved planning to optimized resource allocation and risk mitigation. Real-life case studies bring these concepts to life, offering tangible examples for you to relate to.

Identifying Challenges: No journey is without its challenges. In this book, we dissect the common obstacles faced by Sales Managers, ranging from incomplete data to market uncertainties. Through practical insights and case studies, we guide you in overcoming these hurdles.

Key Points and Best Practices: Learn the key points to keep in mind when forecasting, emphasizing data quality, continuous market analysis, and cross-functional collaboration. Practical examples and actionable strategies will empower you to implement these best practices in your organization.

Methods and Techniques: Uncover various methods and techniques employed in sales forecasting, from qualitative methods to advanced machine learning models. Detailed explanations and examples will guide you through the application of each method.

Step-by-Step Guidance: Navigate the forecasting process step by step, from defining objectives to validation and adjustment processes. Templates and action plans provide practical tools to implement these steps effectively.

Validation and Continuous Improvement: Validate your forecasts against industry standards, engage in scenario analysis, and establish continuous improvement mechanisms. These chapters provide the crucial elements for refining your forecasting processes over time.

Addressing Forecasting Challenges: Dedicated to addressing key forecasting challenges, this section explores the pitfalls of overreliance on historical data, ignoring qualitative factors, and more. Actionable solutions and strategies will help you steer clear of these challenges.

Conclusion: As we conclude this journey, we recap key insights, underline the continuous evolution of sales forecasting, and encourage you to embrace ongoing learning and adaptation. Action plans and templates provide tangible tools for your continuous improvement.

Appendix: Finally, discover a treasure trove of templates and tools in the appendix. These practical resources will aid in the implementation of the concepts discussed throughout the book.

How to Use This Book

This book is designed to be more than a passive read—it's a companion in your professional growth. Engage with the real-life case studies, participate in interactive exercises, and reflect on how each chapter's principles apply to your unique organizational context.

So, whether you're a seasoned professional seeking to refine your forecasting skills or a newcomer eager to grasp the fundamentals, embark on this journey with us. Let's master the art and science of sales forecasting together, shaping a future where strategic decisions are anchored in accurate predictions.

Happy forecasting!

Introduction to Sales Forecasting

Sales forecasting is the cornerstone of strategic planning for businesses, providing a systematic approach to estimating future sales performance. In this chapter, we will explore the fundamental aspects of sales forecasting, from its definition and historical evolution to its contemporary significance in modern business strategy. Additionally, we'll provide an overview of the book's objectives and structure, setting the stage for a comprehensive exploration of practical steps in mastering the art of sales forecasting.

Definition and Scope of Sales Forecasting

Sales forecasting is the process of estimating future sales based on historical data, market trends, and relevant factors influencing consumer behavior. It involves the systematic analysis of past performance to make informed predictions about future sales outcomes. The scope of sales forecasting extends across various industries and business models, encompassing both product and service-oriented enterprises.

Example: Consider a retail business planning for the upcoming holiday season. By analyzing past sales data, customer trends, and external factors like economic conditions, the business can forecast the demand for specific products and optimize inventory levels accordingly.

Historical Evolution of Sales Forecasting

The practice of sales forecasting has evolved over time, adapting to changes in business landscapes and technological advancements. In the early days, businesses relied on simple methods, often intuitive, to predict sales. With the advent of computers and data analytics, more sophisticated forecasting techniques emerged, allowing for a more accurate and data-driven approach.

Example: In the 20th century, businesses predominantly used manual methods such as extrapolation from historical data and simple trend analysis. Today, advanced statistical models and machine learning algorithms enable businesses to analyze vast datasets and identify complex patterns for more accurate predictions.

Significance in Modern Business Strategy

Sales forecasting holds a pivotal role in modern business strategy, influencing decision-making processes at various levels within an organization. It serves as a guiding tool for resource allocation, financial planning, and setting realistic business goals. Accurate sales forecasts empower businesses to respond proactively to market changes, optimize inventory management, and stay competitive in dynamic environments.

Example: A tech company planning the launch of a new product can use sales forecasting to estimate the potential market demand, allocate marketing budgets effectively, and optimize production schedules to meet customer expectations.

Overview of the Book's Objectives and Structure

Objectives: The primary objectives of this book are to empower Sales Managers and business leaders with the knowledge and skills to master sales forecasting. It aims to provide practical insights, actionable steps, and a holistic understanding of the various aspects involved in creating accurate sales forecasts.

Structure: The book is structured to guide readers through a logical progression, starting from foundational concepts and challenges to advanced forecasting methods and validation techniques. Each chapter builds on the previous one, offering a comprehensive and practical approach to mastering the art of sales forecasting.

Action Plan and Templates: Throughout the book, readers will find actionable steps, real-world examples, and templates to facilitate the application of concepts. These tools are designed to help readers implement the principles discussed in each chapter, turning theoretical knowledge into practical skills.

Example: In later chapters, we will provide templates for data gathering, forecasting methods, and validation processes. These templates will serve as practical tools that readers can customize for their specific business needs.

Reflection Prompts:

Reflect on Your Organization:

- ✓ How is sales forecasting currently approached in your organization?
- ✓ Are there specific challenges or gaps in the existing forecasting process?

Setting Objectives:

- ✓ What objectives would you set for improving sales forecasting in your organization?
- ✓ How can the principles introduced in this chapter contribute to achieving those objectives?

Structuring Your Approach:

- ✓ Consider the structure of your organization. How might the principles of sales forecasting be adapted to fit within your organizational structure?

By the end of this book, readers will not only understand the importance of sales forecasting but will also possess the skills and knowledge necessary to create reliable and accurate sales forecasts that drive business success.

Importance of Forecasting in Business

Sales forecasting serves as a linchpin in the strategic planning of businesses, wielding a profound impact on various facets of organizational decision-making, financial planning, and overall success. In this chapter, we will delve into the critical role that sales forecasting plays in shaping strategic initiatives, influencing decision-making processes, and contributing to the overall success of an organization.

The Role of Sales Forecasting in Strategic Planning

Sales forecasting is the bedrock of effective strategic planning, providing businesses with a forward-looking perspective on market dynamics and consumer behavior. By accurately predicting future sales, organizations can align their objectives, allocate resources efficiently, and proactively respond to market trends. This strategic foresight enables businesses to set realistic goals and benchmarks, fostering a more targeted and purposeful approach to growth.

Example: Consider a fashion retailer looking to expand its product line. Through sales forecasting, the retailer can identify emerging trends, estimate demand for specific styles, and strategically plan inventory levels and marketing efforts to capitalize on the forecasted demand.

Impact on Decision-Making Processes

Informed decision-making is contingent upon accurate and reliable data, and sales forecasting provides precisely that. The insights garnered from forecasting enable executives and decision-makers to make sound choices in areas such as marketing strategies, product development, and resource allocation. Whether it's deciding on the launch of a new product or adjusting marketing budgets, sales forecasts serve as a compass for strategic decision-making.

Example: A software company, using sales forecasting, can decide whether to invest in the development of new features based on projected customer demand. This data-driven decision ensures that resources are allocated to areas that align with market needs.

Relationship with Financial Planning and Budgeting

Sales forecasting is intimately intertwined with financial planning and budgeting processes. Accurate sales predictions provide the foundation for developing realistic financial plans, setting revenue targets, and establishing budgets for various business functions. This alignment between sales forecasting and financial planning ensures that financial resources are allocated judiciously, minimizing the risk of overspending or underinvesting.

Example: A manufacturing company, incorporating sales forecasts into its financial planning, can determine production budgets, raw material procurement plans, and staffing levels to meet anticipated demand while optimizing costs.

Contributions to Overall Organizational Success

The ultimate goal of any business is sustained success and growth. Sales forecasting contributes significantly to achieving this goal by providing a roadmap for navigating market challenges and capitalizing on opportunities. When integrated seamlessly into the organizational fabric, sales forecasting becomes a catalyst for improved operational efficiency, customer satisfaction, and competitive advantage.

Example: An e-commerce platform, leveraging sales forecasts, can tailor its user experience, marketing campaigns, and inventory management to meet the evolving demands of its customer base. This adaptability contributes to customer satisfaction and long-term business success.

Action Plans and Templates

Throughout this chapter, readers will find actionable insights and templates to integrate sales forecasting into strategic planning, decision-making processes, and financial planning. These practical tools aim to guide businesses in implementing a systematic approach to sales forecasting, ensuring that the principles discussed in this chapter can be translated into tangible actions.

Reflection Prompts:

Aligning with Strategic Goals:

- ✓ Reflect on your organization's strategic goals. How can sales forecasting contribute to achieving these goals?
- ✓ Are there specific decision-making processes where improved forecasting could have a significant impact?

Financial Implications:

- ✓ Consider the relationship between sales forecasting and financial planning in your organization.
- ✓ How can a more accurate sales forecast positively influence budgeting and resource allocation?

Overall Organizational Success:

- ✓ Reflect on instances where accurate forecasting has directly contributed to your organization's overall success.
- ✓ In what ways can you leverage forecasting to further enhance organizational performance?

By recognizing the pivotal role of sales forecasting in strategic planning, decision-making, and financial management, businesses can leverage this powerful tool to not only survive in dynamic markets but to thrive and achieve enduring success.

Why Accurate Forecasting is Crucial for Sales Managers

In the dynamic landscape of sales management, accurate forecasting is not just a tool; it's a strategic imperative that empowers Sales Managers to fulfill their multifaceted responsibilities. This chapter explores the critical role that precise sales forecasting plays in the day-to-day activities and long-term success of Sales Managers.

The Responsibilities of Sales Managers

Sales Managers are entrusted with a myriad of responsibilities, ranging from overseeing sales teams and setting performance targets to developing and implementing sales strategies. At the core of these responsibilities lies the need for foresight and strategic planning. Accurate sales forecasting equips Sales Managers with the insights needed to navigate the complexities of the market, anticipate trends, and make informed decisions.

Example: Imagine a Sales Manager in the pharmaceutical industry responsible for launching a new drug. Accurate sales forecasting allows them to project demand, optimize distribution channels, and allocate resources effectively, ensuring a successful product launch.

Dependence on Accurate Forecasts for Decision-Making

The decision-making processes of Sales Managers are intrinsically linked to the accuracy of sales forecasts. Whether it's deciding on inventory levels, adjusting pricing strategies, or launching new products, Sales Managers rely on forecasted data to make decisions that impact the overall performance of their teams and contribute to the company's bottom line.

Example: A Sales Manager in a software company, using accurate sales forecasts, can make data-driven decisions on the allocation of sales territories, salesforce training, and promotional activities, maximizing the team's effectiveness in reaching revenue targets.

Setting Realistic Quotas and Targets

One of the primary responsibilities of Sales Managers is to set achievable sales quotas and targets for their teams. Accurate sales forecasting is the linchpin of this process, allowing managers to establish goals that are both ambitious and attainable. Realistic quotas, based on accurate predictions, motivate sales teams by providing a clear roadmap and instilling a sense of achievement.

Example: Consider a Sales Manager in a retail environment during the holiday season. Accurate forecasting enables them to set realistic sales quotas for individual sales representatives, aligning with expected customer demand and optimizing team performance.

Performance Evaluation and Team Motivation

Sales Managers play a crucial role in evaluating the performance of their teams. Accurate sales forecasts provide a benchmark against which actual performance can be measured. This not only facilitates objective performance evaluations but also serves as a motivational tool for sales teams. When teams achieve or surpass forecasted targets, it fosters a sense of accomplishment and encourages continued excellence.

Example: A Sales Manager in a telecommunications company, utilizing accurate sales forecasts, can assess the performance of sales representatives in achieving monthly targets. Recognizing and rewarding teams that exceed forecasts can boost morale and motivation.

Action Plans and Templates

This chapter offers practical action plans and templates for Sales Managers to integrate accurate sales forecasting into their decision-making processes, quota-setting activities, and performance evaluation strategies. These tools are designed to streamline the integration of forecasting into the daily responsibilities of Sales Managers, ensuring that they can leverage the power of accurate predictions to enhance team performance and achieve organizational goals.

Reflection Prompts:

Assessing Responsibilities:

- ✓ Reflect on your role as a Sales Manager. How dependent are your day-to-day responsibilities on accurate sales forecasts?
- ✓ Are there specific challenges or decisions where improved forecasting would be particularly beneficial?

Setting Realistic Quotas:

- ✓ Consider the process of setting sales quotas. How can accurate forecasting contribute to setting more realistic and achievable targets?
- ✓ Are there past instances where inaccurate forecasts led to unattainable quotas?

Performance Evaluation:

- ✓ Reflect on how performance evaluations are currently conducted in your team.

- ✓ How might accurate forecasting enhance the fairness and effectiveness of performance assessments?

By understanding the indispensable role of accurate forecasting in their multifaceted roles, Sales Managers can proactively harness this strategic tool to make informed decisions, set achievable targets, and inspire their teams to achieve excellence.

Benefits of Reliable and Accurate Sales Forecasting

Accurate sales forecasting is not merely a number-crunching exercise; it is a strategic tool that brings about a myriad of benefits to businesses. In this chapter, we delve into the tangible advantages that reliable and accurate sales forecasting offers, from improving strategic planning to optimizing inventory management and enhancing overall sales performance.

Improved Strategic Planning

Reliable sales forecasting lays the groundwork for improved strategic planning. By providing a forward-looking perspective on market trends and customer behavior, businesses can align their objectives with anticipated market demands. This enables strategic planners to develop more targeted and effective strategies, fostering a proactive approach to growth and competition.

Example: A technology company, leveraging accurate sales forecasts, can strategically plan the development of new products by aligning them with projected market trends, ensuring a competitive edge in the rapidly evolving tech landscape.

Enhanced Resource Allocation

Accurate sales forecasts empower businesses to allocate resources effectively. From personnel to marketing budgets and production capacities, businesses can align their resources with forecasted demand. This optimization minimizes inefficiencies and ensures that resources are directed where they can have the most significant impact on the bottom line.

Example: A manufacturing firm, using reliable sales forecasts, can allocate production resources based on anticipated demand, avoiding overproduction or stockouts and optimizing operational efficiency.

Risk Mitigation and Contingency Planning

One of the crucial benefits of accurate sales forecasting is its role in risk mitigation and contingency planning. By foreseeing potential market shifts or economic uncertainties, businesses can develop contingency plans to navigate challenges effectively. This proactive approach safeguards against unforeseen circumstances that may impact sales performance.

Example: In a retail business, accurate sales forecasting can help anticipate seasonal fluctuations in demand. This insight allows the business to implement contingency plans, such as adjusting inventory levels or promotional strategies, to mitigate the impact of unexpected changes in consumer behavior.

Optimized Inventory Management

Accurate sales forecasts are instrumental in optimizing inventory management. Businesses can align production schedules and stock levels with anticipated demand, preventing overstocking or stockouts. This not only reduces carrying costs but also enhances customer satisfaction by ensuring product availability when and where it is needed.

Example: An e-commerce platform, using accurate sales forecasts, can optimize its inventory management system by adjusting stock levels based on anticipated demand spikes during promotional events or seasonal trends.

Increased Sales Performance

Ultimately, the goal of sales forecasting is to contribute to increased sales performance. By setting realistic and achievable targets informed by accurate forecasts, businesses can motivate sales teams to excel. Sales representatives are empowered with clear goals, fostering a sense of purpose and direction that positively impacts their performance.

Example: A Sales Manager, armed with accurate sales forecasts, can set performance targets that challenge sales representatives without being unattainable. This approach motivates the team to meet and exceed expectations, contributing to increased overall sales performance.

Action Plans and Templates

Throughout this chapter, readers will find practical action plans and templates to implement the benefits of reliable and accurate sales forecasting. These tools are designed to guide businesses in integrating forecasting into their strategic planning, resource allocation, risk management, and inventory optimization processes.

Reflection Prompts:

Strategic Planning Improvements:

- ✓ Consider the strategic planning process in your organization. In what ways can improved forecasting positively impact strategic decision-making?
- ✓ Are there examples where strategic plans were negatively affected by inaccurate forecasts?

Resource Allocation Challenges:

- ✓ Reflect on past challenges related to resource allocation.

- ✓ How might enhanced forecasting contribute to more effective allocation of resources?

Risk Mitigation Strategies:

- ✓ Consider instances where unforeseen risks impacted your organization.
- ✓ How can reliable forecasting be integrated into risk mitigation and contingency planning?

Challenges in Accurate Sales Forecasting

Sales forecasting, while a powerful tool, comes with its set of challenges that Sales Managers must navigate to achieve precision in predictions. In this chapter, we explore the common hurdles faced in accurate sales forecasting, ranging from data challenges to uncertainties in market conditions, and provide insights on overcoming these obstacles.

Incomplete or Inaccurate Data

A significant challenge in sales forecasting is the reliance on incomplete or inaccurate data. Inaccuracies in historical sales data or gaps in the data collection process can compromise the accuracy of forecasts. This challenge is particularly pronounced in industries where data collection mechanisms are not standardized or where there are inconsistencies in reporting.

Example: A retail business, relying on sales data from multiple channels with varying reporting formats, may face challenges in aggregating and analyzing data accurately, leading to incomplete or inaccurate forecasting inputs.

Action Plan: Implement robust data validation processes and invest in data cleansing tools to ensure the accuracy and completeness of historical sales data. Establish clear data collection protocols across all relevant channels to minimize discrepancies.

Market Volatility and Uncertainties

The dynamic nature of markets introduces volatility and uncertainties that challenge accurate forecasting. External factors such as economic shifts, geopolitical events, or sudden changes in consumer behavior can disrupt established patterns, making it difficult to predict future sales with precision.

Example: An automotive manufacturer may face challenges in forecasting sales accurately if market uncertainties, such as changes in fuel prices or regulatory policies, significantly impact consumer preferences and purchasing behavior.

Action Plan: Implement scenario analysis techniques to assess the impact of various market scenarios on sales forecasts. Stay abreast of industry trends and economic indicators to adapt forecasts dynamically in response to changing market conditions.

Inadequate Technology and Tools

Outdated or inadequate technology and tools hinder the accuracy of sales forecasting. Legacy systems may lack the capability to process large datasets efficiently or incorporate advanced forecasting techniques. Inadequate tools limit the ability to harness the full potential of available data for precise predictions.

Example: A tech company relying on outdated forecasting software may struggle to incorporate machine learning algorithms or advanced statistical models, limiting the accuracy and sophistication of its sales forecasts.

Action Plan: Invest in state-of-the-art forecasting tools and technologies that can handle large datasets and leverage advanced algorithms. Provide training to the team on the effective use of these tools to maximize their capabilities.

Case Studies on Common Obstacles Faced by Sales Managers

In-depth case studies on common obstacles faced by Sales Managers offer real-world insights into the challenges of accurate sales forecasting. These case studies provide practical examples of how businesses have addressed or succumbed to challenges, offering valuable lessons for readers.

Example: A case study may explore how a consumer electronics company faced challenges in forecasting due to rapidly evolving technology trends, highlighting the importance of adaptability and continuous market analysis in accurate forecasting.

Action Plan: Analyze case studies to identify patterns and successful strategies in overcoming challenges. Extract lessons and apply them to the specific context of your business to enhance the accuracy of sales forecasting.

Action Plans and Templates

This chapter includes actionable insights and templates to help Sales Managers address the challenges of accurate sales forecasting. These tools guide the implementation of strategies to overcome data challenges, navigate market uncertainties, and leverage technology effectively.

Example: A template for developing a data validation process or a checklist for assessing the impact of market uncertainties on forecasts can be provided as practical tools for Sales Managers.

Reflection Prompts:

Data Quality Assessment:

- ✓ Reflect on the quality of data used in your current forecasting process.
- ✓ What steps can be taken to address any issues related to incomplete or inaccurate data?

Market Volatility Preparedness:

- ✓ Consider how your organization responds to market volatility and uncertainties.
- ✓ In what ways can forecasting methodologies be adapted to better navigate unpredictable market conditions?

Technology and Tools Evaluation:

- ✓ Reflect on the technology and tools currently utilized for forecasting.
- ✓ How can the challenges related to inadequate technology and tools be addressed?

By acknowledging and proactively addressing these challenges, Sales Managers can fortify their forecasting processes, improving accuracy and resilience in the face of dynamic market conditions.

Key Points to Keep in Mind when Forecasting

Accurate sales forecasting is contingent upon a strategic approach that considers key factors pivotal to the precision of predictions. In this chapter, we explore essential considerations that Sales Managers must keep in mind to enhance the accuracy and reliability of their forecasting processes.

Emphasis on Data Quality

The foundation of any accurate forecast lies in the quality of the data upon which it is built. Inaccurate or incomplete data can significantly compromise the reliability of predictions. Ensuring data accuracy involves validating historical sales data, cleansing datasets, and maintaining consistency in data collection methods.

Example: A technology company aiming to launch a new product may emphasize data quality by ensuring that customer feedback, sales transactions, and market research are accurately recorded and validated before being incorporated into the forecasting model.

Action Plan: Implement data validation processes and invest in data quality tools to identify and rectify inaccuracies. Regularly audit and clean databases to maintain the integrity of historical data, enhancing the reliability of forecasts.

Continuous Market Analysis and Monitoring

Markets are dynamic, and staying attuned to changes is crucial for accurate forecasting. Continuous market analysis involves monitoring industry trends, competitor activities, and external factors that can influence consumer behavior. Regularly updating forecasts based on the latest market insights ensures relevance and precision.

Example: An e-commerce business may engage in continuous market analysis to identify shifts in consumer preferences, emerging competitors, and changes in online shopping behavior, enabling the adjustment of sales forecasts accordingly.

Action Plan: Establish a systematic process for ongoing market analysis, including regular reviews of industry publications, competitor activities, and consumer trends. Integrate feedback loops that allow the forecasting model to adapt dynamically to changing market conditions.

Cross-Functional Collaboration

Collaboration across departments is vital for holistic and accurate forecasting. Sales Managers should actively engage with teams from marketing, finance, and operations to gather diverse perspectives and insights. Cross-functional collaboration ensures that forecasts consider a comprehensive range of factors, contributing to more accurate predictions.

Example: In a retail business, collaboration between the sales and marketing teams can provide valuable insights into the effectiveness of promotional activities and customer responses, enriching the forecasting process.

Action Plan: Establish regular cross-functional meetings or workshops to facilitate collaboration. Develop a shared understanding of each department's role in the forecasting process and encourage open communication to gather insights from different perspectives.

Adaptability to Changing Business Environments

The ability to adapt to changing business environments is critical for effective forecasting. External factors such as economic shifts, technological advancements, or unforeseen events can impact sales performance. Sales Managers must design forecasting models that are flexible and can be adjusted rapidly in response to changing circumstances.

Example: A hospitality business may need to adapt its sales forecasts quickly in response to changes in travel restrictions, economic downturns, or unexpected events such as natural disasters.

Action Plan: Incorporate scenario planning into the forecasting process to anticipate potential changes in business environments. Develop contingency plans that can be activated in response to unforeseen events, ensuring the resilience of the forecasting model.

Action Plans and Templates

This chapter includes practical action plans and templates to implement the key points discussed in forecasting. Templates for data quality checks, market analysis frameworks, collaboration protocols, and adaptability strategies are provided as tools to enhance the effectiveness of the forecasting process.

Example: A template for conducting a comprehensive data quality audit or a guide for setting up a cross-functional collaboration framework can serve as actionable tools for Sales Managers.

Reflection Prompts:

Emphasizing Data Quality:

- ✓ Reflect on the emphasis placed on data quality in your organization's forecasting processes.
- ✓ How can a greater focus on data quality enhance the accuracy of forecasts?

Continuous Market Analysis:

- ✓ Consider the frequency of market analysis in your organization.
- ✓ How can a commitment to continuous market analysis improve the responsiveness of forecasts to changing market conditions?

Cross-Functional Collaboration:

- ✓ Reflect on collaboration practices between different departments involved in forecasting.
- ✓ In what ways can cross-functional collaboration be strengthened to improve overall forecasting effectiveness?

By keeping these key points in mind, Sales Managers can establish a robust foundation for their forecasting processes, fostering accuracy, adaptability, and collaboration that contribute to informed decision-making and overall organizational success.

Methods and Techniques for Sales Forecasting

Sales forecasting employs a diverse range of methods and techniques, each offering unique insights into future sales performance. In this chapter, we explore four key approaches: Qualitative Methods, Time Series Analysis, Regression Analysis, and Machine Learning Models, providing insights into their applications, benefits, and considerations.

1. **Qualitative Methods:** Expert Opinions, Market Research, and Customer Feedback
   Qualitative methods involve subjective inputs, drawing on the expertise of individuals, market research findings, and direct customer feedback. This approach is particularly valuable when historical data is limited or unreliable.
   Example: In a start-up venture, where historical sales data may be scant, qualitative methods can involve gathering insights from industry experts, conducting focus groups, and collecting feedback directly from potential customers to gauge market interest and demand.
   Action Plan: Develop a structured process for gathering qualitative insights, including methods for expert consultations, market research frameworks, and customer feedback mechanisms. Consider creating templates for recording and analyzing qualitative data to ensure consistency and objectivity in the interpretation of insights.

2. **Time Series Analysis:** Patterns and Trends in Historical Data
   Time series analysis involves examining historical sales data to identify patterns, trends, and recurring cycles. This method relies on the assumption that past performance can provide valuable insights into future behavior.
   Example: A retail business can use time series analysis to identify seasonal sales patterns, such as increased demand during holiday seasons, and adjust forecasts accordingly. This approach allows businesses to anticipate and capitalize on recurring trends.
   Action Plan: Create a time series analysis template that includes data visualization tools to identify patterns and trends. Implement statistical techniques to decompose time series data into its components, such as seasonality and trend, facilitating a more accurate understanding of historical sales behavior.
3. **Regression Analysis**: Understanding Relationships with Other Variables
   Regression analysis explores the relationships between sales and other relevant variables, such as marketing expenditures, economic indicators, or demographic data. By identifying correlations, businesses can gain insights into the factors influencing sales performance.
   Example: A technology company might use regression analysis to assess the impact of marketing spending on product sales. This can help optimize marketing budgets by

identifying the most effective strategies for driving sales.

Action Plan: Develop a regression analysis framework, specifying the variables to be analyzed and the statistical methods to be applied. Create templates for data collection and analysis to streamline the regression modeling process. Ensure that the chosen variables align with the specific dynamics of the business.

4. **Machine Learning Models:** Advanced Algorithms for Complex Patterns

   Machine learning models leverage advanced algorithms to analyze vast datasets and identify complex patterns that may elude traditional methods. These models can adapt and learn from new data, making them well-suited for dynamic and complex forecasting environments.

   Example: An e-commerce platform might employ machine learning algorithms to analyze customer behavior, purchase history, and external factors. The model can then predict future sales patterns with a high degree of accuracy, adapting to changes in consumer preferences.

   Action Plan: Invest in machine learning tools or collaborate with data scientists to implement advanced algorithms. Develop a process for training and validating machine learning models, ensuring that they align with the specific forecasting needs of the business. Create templates for data preprocessing and model evaluation to streamline the implementation of machine learning techniques.

Action Plans and Templates

This chapter includes practical action plans and templates to guide the implementation of each forecasting method. Templates for expert consultation frameworks, time series analysis tools, regression modeling guides, and machine learning implementation plans are provided to assist Sales Managers in integrating these techniques into their forecasting processes.

Example: A template for conducting a qualitative market research survey or a guide for implementing a machine learning algorithm can serve as actionable tools for Sales Managers.

Reflection Prompts:

Qualitative Methods Integration:

- ✓ Reflect on the use of qualitative methods in your current forecasting approach.
- ✓ How can expert opinions, market research, or customer feedback be more effectively integrated into the forecasting process?

Time Series and Regression Analysis Evaluation:

- ✓ Consider the use of time series and regression analysis in your organization.
- ✓ How might these methods be refined or expanded to capture more accurate trends and relationships?

Exploring Advanced Models:

- ✓ Reflect on the level of sophistication in your organization's forecasting models.
- ✓ In what ways could advanced machine learning models be explored to uncover complex patterns?

By understanding the nuances of each method and employing a judicious combination based on the specific context of the business, Sales Managers can enhance the precision and effectiveness of their sales forecasting processes.

How to Forecast Step by Step

Accurate sales forecasting is a systematic process that involves several key steps. In this chapter, we break down the process into a comprehensive, step-by-step guide, from defining objectives to validating and adjusting forecasts.

Defining Objectives and Scope

The first step in the forecasting process is to define clear objectives and scope. What are the specific goals of the forecast? Is it to predict overall sales, assess the impact of marketing campaigns, or anticipate the demand for specific products? Establishing the objectives and scope provides a roadmap for the entire forecasting process.

Example: For a beverage company launching a new product, the objective could be to forecast the sales volume of the new product in the first quarter, considering factors like marketing efforts, seasonality, and consumer preferences.

Action Plan: Create a template for defining forecasting objectives and scope, including key questions to address. Ensure that stakeholders from relevant departments contribute to this initial planning phase to capture diverse perspectives.

Data Gathering and Analysis

Once objectives are defined, the next step is to gather and analyze relevant data. This includes historical sales data, customer feedback, market research, and any other data points crucial for the specific forecasting goals. The quality and comprehensiveness of the data play a pivotal role in the accuracy of the forecast.

Example: A software company aiming to forecast future sales may gather data on previous product launches, customer satisfaction surveys, and market trends in the software industry.

Action Plan: Develop a data gathering plan that outlines the sources, methods, and frequency of data collection. Create templates for data storage and ensure data quality checks are incorporated into the process to maintain the integrity of the dataset.

Selection of Forecasting Method

Choosing the right forecasting method is a critical decision that depends on the nature of the data and the objectives of the forecast. Qualitative methods, time series analysis, regression analysis, or machine learning models may be employed based on the specific requirements of the forecast.

Example: A fashion retailer may choose time series analysis to predict sales for seasonal clothing items, leveraging historical sales data to identify patterns and trends.

Action Plan: Develop a decision-making framework for selecting the appropriate forecasting method. Consider factors such as the availability of historical data, the level of complexity in the relationships between variables, and the specific goals of the forecast.

Developing the Forecast

With the chosen method in place, the next step is to develop the forecast. This involves applying the selected forecasting technique to the gathered data to generate predictions. The output may include numerical estimates, graphical representations, or other formats depending on the chosen method.

Example: Using regression analysis, a manufacturing company may develop a forecast that predicts sales based on variables such as production capacity, advertising expenditures, and economic indicators.

Action Plan: Create a forecasting model based on the chosen method. Develop templates for visualizing and presenting the forecasted data. Ensure that the model is flexible enough to adapt to changes in data inputs or market conditions.

Validation and Adjustment Processes

Validation is a crucial step to assess the accuracy of the forecast. Comparing the forecasted values with actual outcomes helps identify any discrepancies and allows for adjustments to the model. This step ensures that the forecast remains relevant and reliable.

Example: A technology company may validate its sales forecast by comparing predicted sales figures for a new product with the actual sales data after the product launch.

Action Plan: Develop a validation framework that includes key performance indicators (KPIs) to assess the accuracy of the forecast. Establish regular review processes to validate the forecast against actual outcomes and adjust the model as needed.

Action Plans and Templates

This chapter includes practical action plans and templates to guide Sales Managers through each step of the forecasting process. Templates for objective definition, data gathering, method selection, forecasting model development, and validation processes are provided as tools to facilitate a systematic and effective forecasting approach.

Example: A template for validating and adjusting forecasts or a guide for selecting the appropriate forecasting method can serve as actionable tools for Sales Managers.

Reflection Prompts:

Defining Objectives and Scope:

- ✓ Reflect on how well forecasting objectives are defined before initiating the process.
- ✓ How can a clearer definition of objectives enhance the effectiveness of forecasting?

Data Gathering Efficiency:

- ✓ Consider the efficiency of data gathering processes in your organization.
- ✓ What improvements can be made to streamline data collection and analysis?

Validation and Adjustment Processes:

- ✓ Reflect on the current validation and adjustment processes in place.
- ✓ How can these processes be refined to ensure continuous improvement in forecasting accuracy?

By following these step-by-step guidelines and leveraging the provided tools, Sales Managers can implement a robust and systematic approach to sales forecasting, enhancing the accuracy and effectiveness of their predictions.

Validating the Forecast

Validating the forecast is a critical step in the sales forecasting process, ensuring that predictions align with actual outcomes and providing insights for continuous improvement. In this chapter, we explore key strategies for validating forecasts, including benchmarking against industry standards, scenario analysis, establishing feedback mechanisms, and fostering continuous improvement.

Benchmarking Against Industry Standards

Benchmarking involves comparing forecasted values with industry standards or benchmarks to assess the accuracy of predictions. This provides context by evaluating performance relative to established norms within the industry.

Example: A software company forecasting sales for a new product can benchmark its predictions against industry benchmarks for similar product launches, considering factors such as adoption rates and market penetration.

Action Plan: Develop a benchmarking framework that identifies relevant industry standards for comparison. Create templates for tracking and analyzing benchmarked data, allowing for a systematic evaluation of forecast accuracy relative to industry norms.

Scenario Analysis for Robust Forecasts

Scenario analysis involves assessing the impact of different scenarios or potential changes on the forecast. By considering various possible outcomes, businesses can enhance the robustness of their forecasts and develop contingency plans for different scenarios.

Example: A retail business, forecasting sales for the upcoming holiday season, may conduct scenario analysis to evaluate the impact of factors such as economic downturns, supply chain disruptions, or unexpected shifts in consumer behavior on sales predictions.

Action Plan: Develop a scenario analysis template that outlines potential scenarios and their impact on the forecast. Establish a process for regularly updating scenarios based on changes in market conditions. Use the insights gained to refine and adjust forecasts as needed.

Establishing Feedback Mechanisms

Feedback mechanisms are essential for continuous improvement in forecasting accuracy. Establishing channels for feedback from various stakeholders, including sales teams, customers, and market analysts, provides valuable insights into the factors influencing forecast accuracy.

Example: A manufacturing company may establish feedback mechanisms by regularly seeking input from sales representatives on factors influencing sales, such as customer preferences, competitor activities, and market trends.

Action Plan: Create feedback mechanisms that allow stakeholders to provide input on forecast accuracy. Develop templates for collecting and analyzing feedback, categorizing insights into areas such as data quality, external factors, or model assumptions. Use feedback to iteratively refine forecasting processes.

Continuous Improvement in Forecasting Accuracy

Continuous improvement involves an ongoing process of refining forecasting methods and models based on insights gained from validation, benchmarking, scenario analysis, and feedback mechanisms. This iterative approach ensures that forecasting processes evolve to meet changing business conditions.

Example: A technology company, using continuous improvement principles, may regularly review and update its machine learning algorithms based on new data inputs, changing market dynamics, and lessons learned from past forecasts.

Action Plan: Incorporate continuous improvement principles into the forecasting process. Establish a regular review cadence to assess the effectiveness of forecasting methods and models. Develop templates for documenting lessons learned and implementing improvements in forecasting accuracy.

Action Plans and Templates

This chapter includes practical action plans and templates to guide Sales Managers through the validation process. Templates for benchmarking analysis, scenario analysis, feedback collection, and continuous improvement plans are provided as tools to facilitate a structured and effective validation approach.

Example: A template for conducting scenario analysis or a guide for establishing feedback mechanisms can serve as actionable tools for Sales Managers.

Reflection Prompts:

Benchmarking Practices:

- ✓ Reflect on whether benchmarking against industry standards is currently practiced.

- ✓ How can benchmarking be more systematically integrated into the validation process?

Scenario Analysis Effectiveness:

- ✓ Consider the effectiveness of scenario analysis in your organization.
- ✓ In what ways can scenario analysis be refined to enhance the robustness of forecasts?

Feedback Mechanism Implementation:

- ✓ Reflect on the presence of feedback mechanisms in your organization.
- ✓ How can feedback channels be improved to capture valuable insights for continuous improvement?

By implementing these strategies and leveraging the provided tools, Sales Managers can establish a robust validation process that enhances the accuracy of sales forecasts and contributes to continuous improvement in forecasting methodologies.

Strategic Opportunity Analysis and Forecast Management

We need to look into the critical process of strategically analyzing opportunities in your sales pipeline and implementing effective forecasting management. This systematic approach ensures a thorough understanding of each opportunity's potential, helping you make informed decisions and enhance the accuracy of your sales forecasts, empowering you to strategically navigate your sales pipeline, recognize warning signs, and mitigate forecast killers for more accurate and successful forecasting.

Section 1: Opportunity Analysis by Essential Metrics

1. Analyze the Opportunity Pipeline Stage
   - ✓ Qualifying, Quote, Demo, Negotiation, Close, etc.
   - ✓ Categorizing opportunities based on their progression through the pipeline.
2. Six Essential Metrics for Opportunity Analysis
   - ✓ *Age:* Assessing the staleness and time pending for each opportunity.
   - ✓ *Size:* Distinguishing between normal and larger deals.
   - ✓ *Effort:* Evaluating your investment in terms of time, visits, and details provided.
   - ✓ *Engagement:* Analyzing the involvement of both you and the customer's stakeholders.
   - ✓ *Stage:* What stage?

- ✓ *Slippage:* Identifying frequent changes in opportunity details like close dates, pricing, specifications, and commitments.

Section 2: Company Averages and Historical Performance

1. Five Averages for Historical Analysis
    - ✓ *Average Sales Cycle for Won Deals:* Understanding the typical duration for successful deals.
    - ✓ *Average Sales Cycle for Lost Deals:* Analyzing how long losing opportunities stay in the pipeline.
    - ✓ *Average Deal Size:* Identifying patterns or ranges for successful deal sizes.
    - ✓ *Average Conversion Rate from Each Stage:* Evaluating conversion rates at different stages.
    - ✓ *Historical Performance of Similar Opportunities:* Assessing how representatives historically handled similar opportunities.

Section 3: Early Warning Signs and Forecast Killers

1. Recognizing Early Warning Signs
    - ✓ Staying close to late-stage opportunities to identify warning signs early on.
    - ✓ Monitoring for slippage, negative velocity, and stalling.
2. Managing Forecast Killers
    - ✓ Identifying characteristics of late-stage opportunities that impact their likelihood of closing.

- ✓ 10 forecast killers (covered in next chapter) to be cautious of, ensuring a more accurate and reliable sales forecast.

By systematically applying these steps, you not only gain a granular understanding of each opportunity but also develop the foresight to manage your sales forecasts effectively.

Identifying and Managing Forecast Killers

We will now explore the critical aspect of identifying and managing forecast killers—elements that can significantly impact the accuracy and reliability of your sales forecast. By understanding and addressing these forecast killers, you can refine your forecasting process and ensure a more realistic representation of your sales pipeline. Given below are actionable insights and methods for managing these forecast killers, contributing to a more reliable and effective sales forecasting process.

1. Understanding Forecast Killers

Timing Challenges

- ✓ Identifying late-stage opportunities that linger beyond the average sales cycle.
- ✓ Implementing flags for opportunities requiring closer scrutiny.

Deal Size Dynamics

- ✓ Analyzing the impact of deal sizes exceeding 3x the company's average.
- ✓ Flagging or removing opportunities with higher conversion challenges.

Slippage Indicators

- ✓ Recognizing frequent close-date changes and sales-price adjustments.
- ✓ Implementing measures to address and manage slippage challenges.

Section 2: Engagement and Progression Signals

2. Stalled Engagement

- ✓ Monitoring customer engagement gaps of several weeks.

- ✓ Strategies for re-engagement and considerations for removing stalled opportunities.

Late-Stage Considerations

- ✓ Counting opportunities that have reached the bottom of the sales funnel.
- ✓ Assessing the likelihood of conversion for opportunities at different stages.

Negative Velocity

- ✓ Recognizing opportunities stalling or regressing in the late stages.
- ✓ Removing opportunities with negative velocity to maintain forecast accuracy.

3. Decision-Making and External Factors

Authority Evaluation

- ✓ Assessing opportunities lacking engagement with decision-makers.
- ✓ Flagging or removing opportunities without access to key decision-makers.

Lead Source Analysis

- ✓ Understanding variations in historical win rates based on lead sources.
- ✓ Adjusting forecasts based on the varying conversion probabilities associated with different lead sources.

Competitor Comparison

- ✓ Evaluating opportunities where the customer hasn't compared products.
- ✓ Reviewing and adjusting the forecast for opportunities lacking competitor analysis.

Late Random Additions

- ✓ Identifying large, last-minute additions exceeding twice the average deal size.
- ✓ Flagging such additions as potentially at-risk and subjecting them to additional scrutiny.

By addressing these ten forecast killers with a proactive and strategic approach, you not only enhance the accuracy of your forecasts but also ensure that your sales pipeline is focused on opportunities with higher conversion potential.

Sales Forecasting Template

This template provides a systematic approach to analyze and forecast sales, incorporating essential metrics, historical averages, and frameworks for early warning signs and forecast killers. Use this tool to enhance the accuracy of your sales projections and make informed decisions in your sales pipeline management.

Keeping in mind the Customers in your pipeline from Enquiry/Lead to Close, use the following Steps to project next month's/next Quarter Sales:

Customer Information:

- ✓ Customer: [Customer Name]
- ✓ Pipeline Stage: [Enquiry/Lead/Qualifying/Quote/Demo/Negotiation/Close]

Analysis Using 6 Metrics:

- ✓ Age: [Age of the opportunity]
- ✓ Size: [Deal size - Normal/Bigger]
- ✓ Effort: [Your time/visits/details provided]
- ✓ Engagement: [Engagement level by both you and the customer's stakeholders]
- ✓ Stage: [Current stage in the sales pipeline]
- ✓ Slippage: [Any frequent changes in opportunity details like close dates, pricing, specifications, commitments, etc.]

Company's 5 Averages:

Won Deals:

- ✓ *Average Sales Cycle:* [Duration for successful deals]
- ✓ *Average Deal Size:* [Pattern or range for successful deal sizes]

- ✓ *Average Conversion Rate from Each Stage:* [Conversion rates at different stages]

Lost Deals:

- ✓ *Average Sales Cycle:* [Duration losing opportunities stay in the pipeline]
- ✓ *Average Deal Size:* [Pattern or range for deal sizes that are less likely to close]

BANT Framework:

- ✓ Budget: [Customer's budget for the opportunity]
- ✓ Authority: [Decision-makers involved]
- ✓ Need: [Customer's specific needs]
- ✓ Timeline: [Expected timeline for closing the deal]

Early Warning Signs:

- ✓ *Stalled Engagement:* [Customer not engaged for a few weeks]
- ✓ *Negative Velocity:* [Opportunities stalling or moving backward in the late stages]
- ✓ *Slippage:* [Frequent close-date pushes and sales-price changes]

Forecast Killers:

- ✓ Timing Challenges: [Opportunities lingering beyond the average sales cycle]
- ✓ Deal Size Dynamics: [Deals exceeding 3x the company's average sales price]
- ✓ Slippage Indicators: [Frequent close-date changes and sales-price adjustments]
- ✓ Stalled Engagement: [Customer engagement gaps of several weeks]
- ✓ Late-Stage Considerations: [Opportunities reaching the bottom of the sales funnel]
- ✓ Negative Velocity: [Opportunities stalling or regressing in the late stages]

- ✓ Authority Evaluation: [Opportunities lacking engagement with decision-makers]
- ✓ Lead Source Analysis: [Variations in historical win rates based on lead sources]
- ✓ Competitor Comparison: [Opportunities lacking competitor analysis]
- ✓ Late Random Additions: [Large, last-minute additions exceeding twice the average deal size]

Note: Customize the template fields with specific details for each customer opportunity in your pipeline.

Overcoming Key Forecasting Challenges

Effective sales forecasting requires overcoming various challenges that can impede accuracy and hinder strategic decision-making. In this chapter, we explore and address four common challenges faced by Sales Managers: Overreliance on Historical Data, Ignoring Qualitative Factors, Lack of Collaboration Among Departments, and Addressing Inadequate Technology and Tools.

Overreliance on Historical Data

One of the challenges in sales forecasting is an overreliance on historical data. While historical data provides valuable insights, relying solely on past performance may lead to inaccuracies, especially in dynamic and rapidly changing markets.

Example: A retail business, solely using historical sales data to forecast demand, may overlook emerging consumer trends or shifts in preferences that are not reflected in past performance.

Action Plan: Develop a template for conducting regular reviews of forecasting methodologies to assess the balance between historical data and forward-looking indicators. Encourage the integration of real-time data, market intelligence, and qualitative insights into the forecasting process.

Ignoring Qualitative Factors

Another challenge is the tendency to overlook qualitative factors in favor of quantitative data. Qualitative insights, such as expert opinions, customer feedback, and market sentiment, are valuable contributors to accurate forecasting.

Example: A technology company may ignore qualitative factors like customer feedback on usability or the reputation of competitors, leading to a less nuanced and potentially inaccurate sales forecast.

Action Plan: Create a template for systematically incorporating qualitative factors into the forecasting process. Establish frameworks for expert consultations, customer feedback collection, and market sentiment analysis to complement quantitative data.

Lack of Collaboration Among Departments

Forecasting challenges often arise when there is a lack of collaboration among different departments within an organization. Sales Managers must work closely with marketing, finance, and operations to gather diverse perspectives and ensure a comprehensive understanding of the factors influencing sales.

Example: In a manufacturing company, if the sales team operates in isolation from the production and finance teams, it may result in inaccurate forecasts due to a lack of insights into production constraints and financial considerations.

Action Plan: Develop a cross-functional collaboration template that outlines key touch points and collaboration protocols. Schedule regular meetings or workshops to facilitate communication and information exchange among departments, ensuring a holistic approach to forecasting.

Addressing Inadequate Technology and Tools

Inadequate technology and tools can hinder the effectiveness of sales forecasting. Outdated systems may lack the capabilities needed for advanced analysis, leading to suboptimal forecasting outcomes.

Example: A retail business using outdated forecasting software may struggle to incorporate machine learning algorithms or analyze large datasets efficiently, limiting the sophistication and accuracy of forecasts.

Action Plan: Create a technology assessment template to evaluate the current forecasting tools and identify areas for improvement. Invest in state-of-the-art forecasting tools that align with the organization's needs and provide training to ensure the effective use of these tools.

Action Plans and Templates

This chapter includes practical action plans and templates to guide Sales Managers in addressing these forecasting challenges. Templates for assessing the balance between historical and forward-looking indicators, incorporating qualitative factors, fostering cross-functional collaboration, and evaluating technology and tools are provided as tools to facilitate effective solutions.

Example: A template for conducting a technology assessment or a guide for establishing cross-functional collaboration can serve as actionable tools for Sales Managers.

Reflection Prompts:

Balancing Historical and Forward-looking Indicators:

- ✓ Reflect on the balance between historical and forward-looking indicators in your forecasting models.
- ✓ How can this balance be adjusted to improve the adaptability of forecasts?

Qualitative Factor Incorporation:

- ✓ Consider the integration of qualitative factors in your forecasting process.
- ✓ In what ways can qualitative insights be more systematically incorporated into models?

Collaboration Enhancement:

- ✓ Reflect on collaboration practices between departments involved in forecasting.
- ✓ How can collaboration be enhanced to address challenges related to communication and information exchange?

By proactively addressing these challenges and implementing the provided action plans, Sales Managers can foster a more resilient and accurate forecasting process, ultimately contributing to informed decision-making and organizational success.

Appendix: Templates and Tools for Practical Implementation

In this appendix, you'll find a collection of templates and tools designed to facilitate the practical implementation of key concepts discussed throughout the book. These resources aim to assist Sales Managers in applying the insights from each chapter to their specific forecasting processes. Sales Managers can customize and implement these resources to suit the specific needs of their organizations, fostering a structured and effective approach to sales forecasting. By leveraging these tools, Sales Managers can navigate challenges, enhance accuracy, and contribute to the ongoing success of their forecasting processes.

Let's explore the templates and tools available:

1. Data Quality Audit Template

Maintaining data accuracy is foundational to reliable forecasting. This template provides a structured framework for conducting a comprehensive data quality audit. It includes sections for assessing data completeness, consistency, and validity, ensuring that the data used in forecasting is reliable and error-free.

Action Plan:

- ✓ Schedule regular data quality audits to identify and rectify inaccuracies.
- ✓ Implement data validation processes based on the findings from the audit.
- ✓ Use the template to document audit results and track improvements over time.

Data Quality Audit Template

Objective: Ensure the accuracy, completeness, and reliability of data in your sales forecasting process.

Section 1: General Information

- ✓ Date of Audit:
- ✓ Auditor:
- ✓ Data Set or Source:

Section 2: Data Accuracy Assessment

- ✓ Customer Information:
  - *Fields:* [List of customer data fields]
  - *Accuracy Rating (1-5):* [Rate the accuracy of each field, 1 being highly inaccurate and 5 being highly accurate]
  - *Comments:*
- ✓ Pipeline Stage Information:
  - *Fields:* [List of pipeline stage-related fields]
  - *Accuracy Rating (1-5):*
  - *Comments:*
- ✓ Deal Size Information:
  - *Fields:* [List of deal size-related fields]
  - *Accuracy Rating (1-5):*
  - *Comments:*

Section 3: Data Completeness Assessment

- ✓ Customer Information:
  - *Fields:* [List of customer data fields]
  - *Completeness Rating (1-5):* [Rate the completeness of each field, 1 being highly incomplete and 5 being highly complete]
  - *Comments:*
- ✓ Pipeline Stage Information:
  - *Fields:* [List of pipeline stage-related fields]
  - *Completeness Rating (1-5):*

- *Comments:*

✓ Deal Size Information:

- *Fields:* [List of deal size-related fields]
- *Completeness Rating (1-5):*
- *Comments:*

Section 4: Data Reliability Assessment

✓ Customer Information:

- *Fields:* [List of customer data fields]
- *Reliability Rating (1-5):* [Rate the reliability of each field, 1 being highly unreliable and 5 being highly reliable]
- *Comments:*

✓ Pipeline Stage Information:

- *Fields:* [List of pipeline stage-related fields]
- *Reliability Rating (1-5):*
- *Comments:*

✓ Deal Size Information:

- *Fields:* [List of deal size-related fields]
- *Reliability Rating (1-5):*
- *Comments:*

Section 5: Overall Data Quality Summary

✓ *Overall Data Accuracy Rating (1-5):* [Calculate an average accuracy rating based on the assessments]

✓ *Overall Data Completeness Rating (1-5):* [Calculate an average completeness rating based on the assessments]

✓ *Overall Data Reliability Rating (1-5):* [Calculate an average reliability rating based on the assessments]

✓ *General Comments and Recommendations:*

Section 6: Action Plan for Improvement

✓ *Identified Issues:* [List any identified data issues]

- ✓ *Recommended Actions:* [Suggest specific actions to address the identified issues]
- ✓ *Responsible Party:* [Specify the individual or team responsible for implementing the recommended actions]
- ✓ *Timeline for Implementation:* [Set deadlines for the completion of each recommended action]

Section 7: Follow-Up

- ✓ *Date of Follow-Up Audit:*
- ✓ *Results of Follow-Up Audit:*
- ✓ *Additional Actions Required:*
- ✓ *Timeline for Additional Actions:* [Set deadlines for any additional actions identified during the follow-up audit]

Note: Customize the template to fit the specific data fields and requirements of your sales forecasting process. Regularly conduct data quality audits to maintain the accuracy and reliability of your sales data.

2. Scenario Analysis Framework

Scenario analysis is a powerful tool for assessing the impact of different situations on sales forecasts. This framework guides Sales Managers through the process of identifying potential scenarios, analyzing their implications, and adjusting forecasts accordingly.

Action Plan:

- ✓ Regularly update scenarios based on changes in market conditions.
- ✓ Incorporate insights from scenario analysis into the forecasting model.
- ✓ Use the framework to create contingency plans for different scenarios.

Scenario Analysis Framework Template

Objective: Evaluate the impact of various scenarios on sales forecasts to make informed decisions.

Section 1: Scenario Identification

- ✓ Scenario Name:
  Description: [Provide a brief description of the scenario]
- ✓ Scenario Variables:
  List of Variables: [Identify the key variables affecting the scenario, e.g., economic conditions, market trends, competitor actions]

Section 2: Assumptions and Inputs

- ✓ Assumptions:
  List of Assumptions: [Document any assumptions made for the scenario]
- ✓ Inputs:
  Data Inputs Required: [Specify the data inputs needed for the scenario analysis]

Section 3: Scenario Development

- ✓ Scenario Timeline:
  Start Date:
  End Date:
- ✓ Scenario Description:
  Narrative: [Provide a narrative describing the scenario, including any relevant background information]
- ✓ Scenario Assumptions:
  Variables: [Specify how each identified variable behaves in this scenario]
  Impact on Sales Forecasts: [Quantify the expected impact on sales forecasts]

Section 4: Data and Model Adjustments

- ✓ Data Adjustments:

Specific Data Adjustments: [Detail any adjustments made to historical or current data to accommodate the scenario]

- ✓ Model Adjustments:

  Adjustments to Forecasting Models: [Specify any modifications to forecasting models considering the scenario]

Section 5: Impact Analysis

- ✓ Sales Forecast Impact:

  Comparison to Baseline: [Compare the scenario's sales forecast to the baseline forecast]

  Percentage Change: [Calculate the percentage change in sales forecasts]

- ✓ Key Performance Indicators (KPIs):

  Identify KPIs: [Specify relevant KPIs affected by the scenario, e.g., conversion rates, deal sizes]

Section 6: Decision Points and Mitigation Strategies

- ✓ Decision Points:

  Identify Decision Points: [Specify crucial decision points influenced by the scenario]

- ✓ Mitigation Strategies:

  Proposed Strategies: [Recommend strategies to mitigate negative impacts or capitalize on positive outcomes]

Section 7: Documentation and Reporting

- ✓ Documentation:

  Data Sources: [List sources of data used for the scenario analysis]

  Methodology: [Describe the methodology followed for the analysis]

- ✓ Reporting:

Format of Reporting: [Specify how the results of the scenario analysis will be presented]
Frequency of Reporting: [Determine how often scenario analysis reports will be generated]

Section 8: Conclusion and Next Steps

Summary of Findings: [Summarize the key findings from the scenario analysis]

Next Steps:

- ✓ *Recommended Actions:* [Suggest any recommended actions based on the scenario analysis]
- ✓ *Responsible Parties:* [Specify individuals or teams responsible for implementing the recommended actions]
- ✓ *Timeline for Implementation:* [Set deadlines for the completion of each recommended action]

Note: Customize the template based on your specific scenario analysis needs, variables, and industry context.

3. Cross-Functional Collaboration Guide

Collaboration among different departments is crucial for holistic forecasting. This guide outlines steps for fostering cross-functional collaboration, including establishing communication protocols, defining roles, and organizing regular meetings.

Action Plan:

- ✓ Implement cross-functional collaboration workshops or training sessions.
- ✓ Develop a shared understanding of each department's role in the forecasting process.
- ✓ Use the guide to create collaboration protocols and improve information exchange.

Cross-Functional Collaboration Guide Template

Objective: Facilitate effective collaboration among different departments for enhanced sales forecasting.

Section 1: Team Information

- ✓ Department:
  List of Departments Involved: [Identify the relevant departments involved in the sales forecasting process]
- ✓ Team Members:
  Roles and Responsibilities: [Specify the roles and responsibilities of each team member]

Section 2: Communication Protocols

- ✓ Communication Channels:
  Primary Communication Channels: [Specify the main channels for inter-departmental communication]
- ✓ Frequency of Communication:
  Regular Meetings: [Determine how often teams will meet to discuss sales forecasting]

Section 3: Data Sharing Guidelines

- ✓ Data Access:
  Specify Data Access Levels: [Define who has access to what data and to what extent]
- ✓ Data Formats:
  Preferred Data Formats: [Agree on standardized formats for sharing data]

Section 4: Collaboration Tools

- ✓ Project Management Tools:
  Selected Tools: [List tools for project management and collaborative work]
- ✓ Communication Platforms:
  Chosen Platforms: [Identify platforms for real-time communication and collaboration]

Section 5: Cross-Functional Meetings

- ✓ Agenda Template:
  Sample Agenda: [Provide a template for the agenda of cross-functional meetings]
- ✓ Meeting Schedule:
  Regular Meeting Schedule: [Determine the regular schedule for cross-functional meetings]

Section 6: Conflict Resolution

- ✓ Conflict Resolution Process:
  Steps to Resolve Conflicts: [Outline a step-by-step process for resolving conflicts]
- ✓ Escalation Protocol:
  When to Escalate: [Specify situations that warrant escalation and the appropriate channels]

Section 7: Training and Knowledge Sharing

- ✓ Training Sessions:
  Planned Training Sessions: [List upcoming training sessions for team members]
- ✓ Knowledge Sharing Platforms:
  Chosen Platforms: [Identify platforms for sharing industry knowledge and insights]

Section 8: Continuous Improvement Mechanisms

- ✓ Feedback Loops:
  Feedback Collection Process: [Define how feedback will be collected from team members]
- ✓ Iterative Improvement:
  Continuous Improvement Initiatives: [Specify ongoing initiatives to enhance collaboration]

Section 9: Roles and Responsibilities Matrix

- ✓ Matrix Template:
  Roles and Responsibilities Matrix: [Provide a matrix outlining roles and responsibilities for each department]

Section 10: Collaboration Success Metrics

- ✓ Key Performance Indicators (KPIs):
  Identified KPIs: [Specify KPIs that measure the success of cross-functional collaboration]
- ✓ Measurement Frequency:
  Frequency of Measurement: [Determine how often KPIs will be measured and assessed]

Note: Customize the template to align with the specific needs, structure, and dynamics of your organization. Regularly revisit and update the guide to ensure its relevance.

4. Technology Assessment Template

Ensuring that technology and tools align with forecasting needs is essential for efficiency. This template facilitates the assessment of existing forecasting tools, identifying strengths, weaknesses, and areas for improvement.

Action Plan:

- ✓ Conduct regular assessments to stay updated on technological advancements.
- ✓ Invest in tools that address identified gaps and enhance forecasting capabilities.
- ✓ Use the template to document the results of technology assessments and guide decision-making.

Technology Assessment Template

Objective: Evaluate the effectiveness of current technologies supporting the sales forecasting process and identify areas for improvement.

Section 1: Current Technology Stack

- ✓ CRM System:
  Vendor:
  Version:
  Key Features Utilized:

- ✓ Forecasting Software:
  Vendor:
  Version:
  Key Features Utilized:
- ✓ Data Analytics Tools:
  Vendor:
  Version:
  Key Features Utilized:
- ✓ Collaboration Platforms:
  Vendor:
  Version:
  Key Features Utilized:

Section 2: User Satisfaction and Feedback

- ✓ User Feedback:
  Collect feedback from end-users on the current technologies
  Identify pain points and areas of satisfaction
- ✓ User Training:
  Assess the effectiveness of current training programs
  Identify any gaps in user knowledge or skill

Section 3: Integration Capabilities

- ✓ Integration with CRM:
  Evaluate how well forecasting software integrates with CRM
  Identify any issues or limitations
- ✓ Data Flow and Connectivity:
  Assess the seamless flow of data between different tools
  Identify any bottlenecks or data silos

Section 4: Data Security and Privacy

- ✓ Data Security Measures:
  Assess the security features of each tool
  Ensure compliance with data privacy regulations

✓ User Access Controls:

Review the access controls in place for sensitive data

Ensure only authorized personnel have access

Section 5: Scalability and Flexibility

✓ Scalability:

Assess the scalability of the current technologies

Evaluate their ability to handle growing data volumes

✓ Adaptability to Changing Needs:

Evaluate how easily the tools can adapt to changes in business requirements

Identify any limitations in flexibility

Section 6: Cost and ROI Analysis

✓ Total Cost of Ownership:

Calculate the total cost of owning and maintaining each technology

Identify any hidden costs

✓ Return on Investment (ROI):

Assess the overall ROI of the current technology stack

Identify areas where ROI can be improved

Section 7: Recommendations and Action Plan

✓ Areas for Improvement:

Identify specific areas where technology enhancements are needed

✓ Technology Upgrade or Replacement:

Recommendations for upgrading or replacing specific tools

Justification for the proposed changes

✓ Implementation Timeline:

Proposed timeline for implementing recommended changes

Consideration of any potential disruptions

Note: Customize the template based on the technologies used in your organization. Regularly revisit and update the assessment to ensure alignment with evolving business needs.

5. Personal Development Plan for Continuous Learning

Continuous learning is key to staying ahead in the field of sales forecasting. This personal development plan template helps Sales Managers set learning goals, identify resources for development, and establish timelines for ongoing improvement.

Action Plan:

- ✓ Set specific learning goals related to forecasting methodologies.
- ✓ Identify relevant courses, conferences, or webinars for skill enhancement.
- ✓ Use the template to track progress and adjust learning goals over time.

Personal Development Plan for Continuous Learning Template

Objective: Facilitate the continuous learning and professional growth of individuals involved in sales forecasting.

Section 1: Personal Goals and Aspirations

- ✓ Career Objectives:
  Short-Term Goals (6-12 months):
  Long-Term Goals (1-3 years):
- ✓ Skills Enhancement:
  Identify specific skills to enhance or acquire:
  Relevant to current role and future aspirations:

Section 2: Current Skill Assessment

- ✓ Self-Assessment:

Rate current proficiency in key skills on a scale of 1-5:

Identify strengths and areas for improvement:

- ✓ Feedback from Managers/Peers:

  Solicit feedback on current skills and performance:

  Identify areas for development based on feedback:

Section 3: Learning Resources and Opportunities

- ✓ Training Programs:

  List relevant training programs or courses:

  Specify the provider, duration, and key focus areas:

- ✓ Workshops and Webinars:

  Identify workshops or webinars to attend:

  Specify the topics and expected learning outcomes:

Section 4: On-the-Job Learning

- ✓ Assignments and Projects:

  Seek opportunities for challenging assignments:

  Projects that align with skill development goals:

- ✓ Mentorship and Coaching:

  Identify potential mentors or coaches:

  Specify areas of expertise to focus on during mentorship:

Section 5: Networking and Collaboration

- ✓ Professional Associations:

  Join relevant professional associations:

  Participate in events and networking opportunities:

- ✓ Collaborative Projects:

  Engage in cross-functional projects:

Collaborate with colleagues to gain diverse perspectives:

Section 6: Progress Tracking and Evaluation

- ✓ Key Performance Indicators (KPIs):
  Define measurable KPIs for skill development:
  Regularly track and assess progress:
- ✓ Feedback and Reflection:
  Solicit feedback from managers, peers, and mentors:
  Reflect on personal growth and areas for adjustment:

Section 7: Time Management and Commitment

- ✓ Allocated Time for Learning:
  Specify the time commitment for learning activities:
  Balance with job responsibilities and personal life:
- ✓ Overcoming Challenges:
  Anticipate potential challenges in the learning journey:
  Outline strategies for overcoming obstacles:

Section 8: Review and Adjustment

- ✓ Review Dates:
  Schedule regular review dates to assess progress:
  Adjust goals and plans based on evolving needs:
- ✓ Flexible Learning Plan:
  Maintain flexibility in the learning plan:
  Adapt to changes in job roles or organizational priorities:

Note: Customize the template according to individual roles, organizational learning resources, and specific career aspirations. Encourage individuals to take ownership of their development plan for continuous learning.

6. Validation and Adjustment Checklist

Validating and adjusting forecasts based on actual outcomes is critical for accuracy. This checklist provides a step-by-step guide for the validation process, ensuring that Sales Managers systematically review and refine their forecasting models.

Action Plan:

- ✓ Regularly compare forecasted values with actual outcomes.
- ✓ Use the checklist to guide the validation process and identify areas for adjustment.
- ✓ Document lessons learned and implement improvements based on the findings.

Validation and Adjustment Checklist Template

Objective: Provide a systematic guide for validating and adjusting sales forecasts for accuracy and reliability.

Section 1: Data Validation

- ✓ Data Completeness:
  Verify that all required data fields are complete
  Address any missing or incomplete information
- ✓ Data Accuracy:
  Cross-check data accuracy against reliable sources
  Correct any inaccuracies in customer information, sales stages, and deal sizes
- ✓ Consistency in Data Formats:
  Ensure consistency in data formats across the forecasting system

Adjust any discrepancies in units, currencies, or other formatting elements

Section 2: Model Validation

- ✓ Accuracy of Forecasting Models:
  Evaluate the accuracy of the chosen forecasting models
  Compare model predictions with actual outcomes
- ✓ Assumption Testing:
  Review and test assumptions made during the forecasting process
  Adjust models based on updated or revised assumptions
- ✓ Scenario Analysis Validation:
  Validate scenarios considered during forecasting against real-world data
  Adjust forecasts based on the impact of validated scenarios

Section 3: External Factors and Market Conditions

- ✓ Market Analysis:
  Review current market conditions and trends
  Adjust forecasts based on external market factors
- ✓ Competitor Analysis:
  Analyze competitor activities and market share
  Adjust forecasts to reflect the competitive landscape
- ✓ Economic Indicators:
  Consider relevant economic indicators affecting the industry
  Adjust forecasts based on the economic outlook

Section 4: Collaboration and Feedback

- ✓ Cross-Functional Feedback:
  Seek feedback from relevant departments (e.g., marketing, sales, finance)
  Incorporate insights and adjustments suggested by cross-functional teams
- ✓ Customer Feedback and Surveys:
  Collect feedback from customers regarding their purchasing intentions
  Adjust forecasts based on customer feedback

Section 5: Historical Performance Review

- ✓ Comparison with Historical Data:
  Compare current forecasts with historical performance data
  Adjust forecasts based on historical trends and patterns
- ✓ Learning from Past Mistakes:
  Identify and address any recurring mistakes or inaccuracies in past forecasts
  Adjust forecasting methodologies to avoid similar issues

Section 6: Sensitivity Analysis

- ✓ Impact of Variable Changes:
  Conduct sensitivity analysis to understand the impact of variable changes
  Adjust forecasts considering different variable scenarios
- ✓ Risk Assessment:
  Assess potential risks that may impact sales forecasts
  Adjust forecasts to include risk mitigation strategies

Section 7: Documentation and Reporting

- ✓ Documentation of Adjustments:
  Document all adjustments made during the validation process

Maintain a record for future reference

- ✓ Reporting to Stakeholders:

  Prepare a summary report highlighting validated adjustments

  Communicate changes to relevant stakeholders

Section 8: Follow-Up and Continuous Improvement

- ✓ Monitoring and Follow-Up:

  Establish a follow-up schedule to monitor the impact of adjustments

  Make additional adjustments as needed

- ✓ Continuous Improvement Initiatives:

  Identify areas for continuous improvement in the forecasting process

  Implement changes to enhance future forecasting accuracy

Note: Customize the template based on the specific forecasting methodologies, data sources, and industry characteristics relevant to your organization.

7. Qualitative Factor Integration Template

Incorporating qualitative factors enriches forecasting insights. This template guides Sales Managers in systematically integrating qualitative data, such as expert opinions and customer feedback, into the forecasting process.

Action Plan:

- ✓ Establish a process for expert consultations and customer feedback collection.
- ✓ Use the template to document qualitative factors and their impact on forecasts.
- ✓ Regularly review and update qualitative inputs to maintain accuracy.

Qualitative Factor Integration Template

Objective: Systematically incorporate qualitative factors into the sales forecasting process for a more comprehensive analysis.

Section 1: Qualitative Factors Identification

- ✓ Market Trends:
  Identify current and emerging market trends relevant to the industry
  Assess the potential impact of these trends on sales
- ✓ Competitive Landscape:
  Analyze the competitive environment and actions of key competitors
  Evaluate how competitor strategies may influence sales forecasts
- ✓ Customer Sentiment:
  Gather feedback and sentiment analysis from customers
  Consider customer perceptions and preferences in forecasting

Section 2: Internal Factors Assessment

- ✓ Product/Service Innovations:
  Assess the impact of new product or service launches on sales
  Consider how innovations may drive or impede sales performance
- ✓ Marketing Initiatives:
  Evaluate the effectiveness of ongoing and planned marketing campaigns
  Consider how marketing efforts may influence customer behavior
- ✓ Sales Team Feedback:

Seek input from the sales team regarding market conditions and challenges

Incorporate insights from the front line into forecasting

Section 3: Industry Regulations and Policies

- ✓ Regulatory Changes:

  Identify any upcoming regulatory changes or policy shifts

  Evaluate how these changes may impact sales forecasts

- ✓ Compliance and Legal Factors:

  Assess the organization's compliance with industry regulations

  Consider legal factors that may affect sales projections

Section 4: Economic Factors Analysis

- ✓ Macro-Economic Indicators:

  Evaluate broader economic indicators such as GDP, inflation, and interest rates

  Consider how macro-economic trends may influence sales

- ✓ Consumer Spending Patterns:

  Analyze patterns in consumer spending and purchasing behavior

  Adjust sales forecasts based on anticipated shifts in spending

Section 5: Integration into Forecasting Models

- ✓ Weighting of Qualitative Factors:

  Assign weights to each identified qualitative factor based on perceived importance

  Determine the influence of each factor on the overall forecast

- ✓ Scoring System:

  Develop a scoring system to quantify the impact of qualitative factors

Establish criteria for assigning scores to different levels of influence

Section 6: Collaborative Analysis

- ✓ Cross-Functional Collaboration:
  Facilitate collaboration between departments (e.g., marketing, sales, operations)
  Engage stakeholders in qualitative factor analysis
- ✓ Expert Opinions:
  Seek expert opinions from individuals with industry-specific knowledge
  Incorporate expert insights into the qualitative analysis

Section 7: Documentation and Reporting

- ✓ Qualitative Factor Summary:
  Document a summary of the qualitative factors considered in forecasting
  Maintain a comprehensive record of qualitative assessments
- ✓ Reporting to Stakeholders:
  Prepare a report highlighting the integration of qualitative factors
  Communicate the impact of qualitative considerations to stakeholders

Note: Customize the template based on the specific qualitative factors relevant to your industry and organization. Regularly update the template to reflect changing market conditions and internal dynamics.

8. Benchmarking Analysis Toolkit

Benchmarking against industry standards provides valuable context for assessing forecast accuracy. This toolkit includes guidelines and tools for conducting benchmarking analyses, helping Sales

Managers compare their performance against established industry norms.

Action Plan:

- ✓ Identify relevant industry benchmarks for comparison.
- ✓ Regularly conduct benchmarking analyses to assess forecast accuracy.
- ✓ Use the toolkit to streamline the benchmarking process and derive actionable insights.

Benchmarking Analysis Toolkit

Objective: Facilitate benchmarking analysis to compare sales forecasting performance against industry standards and peers.

Section 1: Benchmarking Metrics Identification

- ✓ Key Performance Indicators (KPIs):
  Identify relevant KPIs for benchmarking analysis
  Select metrics such as sales growth, conversion rates, and accuracy
- ✓ Industry Standards:
  Research industry benchmarks for sales forecasting
  Identify standard performance metrics for comparison

Section 2: Data Collection and Preparation

- ✓ Internal Data Compilation:
  Gather relevant internal data for benchmarking
  Ensure data consistency and accuracy
- ✓ Peer Benchmarking Data:
  Acquire benchmarking data from industry peers or external sources
  Ensure comparability of data across organizations

Section 3: Comparative Analysis

✓ Performance Scorecard:

Develop a scorecard for comparing performance against benchmarks

Assign scores to different KPIs based on performance levels

✓ Gap Analysis:

Conduct a gap analysis to identify areas of strength and improvement

Compare internal performance with industry benchmarks

Section 4: Root Cause Analysis

✓ Identify Deviations:

Identify areas where internal performance deviates from benchmarks

Determine the root causes of performance variations

✓ Qualitative Analysis:

Include qualitative factors influencing performance

Consider internal and external factors impacting forecasting

Section 5: Action Planning

✓ Performance Improvement Strategies:

Develop strategies to address performance gaps

Define action items for improvement

✓ Best Practices Adoption:

Identify best practices from benchmarking analysis

Implement best practices within the organization

Section 6: Continuous Monitoring

✓ Regular Performance Reviews:

Establish a schedule for regular performance reviews

Monitor progress in closing performance gaps

- ✓ Adaptive Strategies:
  Adapt strategies based on ongoing benchmarking results
  Continuously refine forecasting processes

Section 7: Documentation and Reporting

- ✓ Benchmarking Report:
  Prepare a comprehensive report summarizing benchmarking results
  Include insights, findings, and recommended actions
- ✓ Communication to Stakeholders:
  Communicate benchmarking results to relevant stakeholders
  Highlight areas of improvement and success

Section 8: Knowledge Sharing and Collaboration

- ✓ Cross-Functional Collaboration:
  Facilitate collaboration between different departments based on benchmarking insights
  Encourage knowledge sharing for continuous improvement
- ✓ Benchmarking Forums:
  Participate in industry benchmarking forums
  Contribute to collective learning and improvement

Note: Customize the template based on the specific KPIs and benchmarking criteria relevant to your industry and organization. Regularly update benchmarking analyses to stay informed about evolving industry standards.

9. Continuous Improvement Log

Continuous improvement is an ongoing process that requires systematic tracking of lessons learned and implemented improvements. This log helps Sales

Managers document improvements, assess their impact, and plan for future enhancements.

Action Plan:

- ✓ Establish a regular cadence for reviewing and updating forecasting methodologies.
- ✓ Document lessons learned, changes made, and their outcomes in the log.
- ✓ Use the log to inform future iterations of the forecasting process.

Continuous Improvement Log

Objective: Establish a structured log for recording and tracking continuous improvement initiatives in the sales forecasting process.

Section 1: Improvement Initiatives Identification

- ✓ Opportunity for Improvement:

  Identify specific areas within the sales forecasting process that present opportunities for enhancement

  Consider feedback from stakeholders, performance reviews, and benchmarking results
- ✓ Root Cause Analysis:

  Conduct a root cause analysis to understand the underlying factors contributing to identified issues

  Determine the key drivers of performance gaps or challenges

Section 2: Action Planning and Implementation

- ✓ Action Items:

  Define clear action items to address the identified areas for improvement

  Specify responsible parties and timelines for implementation
- ✓ Resource Allocation:

Allocate necessary resources, including personnel, technology, and training

Ensure that the required resources are readily available

Section 3: Monitoring and Evaluation

- ✓ Implementation Tracking:

  Track the progress of each improvement initiative through various stages of implementation

  Regularly update the log with status reports

- ✓ Key Performance Indicators (KPIs):

  Define KPIs to measure the impact of improvement initiatives

  Establish benchmarks for success and continuous monitoring

Section 4: Feedback and Adaptation

- ✓ Stakeholder Feedback:

  Solicit feedback from relevant stakeholders involved in the improvement initiatives

  Consider feedback to make real-time adjustments as needed

- ✓ Adaptive Strategies:

  Be prepared to adapt strategies based on feedback and changing circumstances

  Update the log with any modifications to the original improvement plan

Section 5: Documentation and Reporting

- ✓ Detailed Documentation:

  Maintain detailed documentation for each improvement initiative, including objectives, strategies, and outcomes

  Create a comprehensive record for future reference

- ✓ Performance Reports:

Generate regular performance reports summarizing the impact of improvement initiatives
Communicate successes and areas for further attention

Section 6: Lessons Learned

- ✓ Successes and Achievements:
  Document successes and achievements resulting from improvement initiatives
  Identify best practices and strategies that led to positive outcomes
- ✓ Challenges and Lessons:
  Document challenges encountered during the improvement process
  Extract lessons learned to inform future initiatives

Section 7: Knowledge Sharing and Training

- ✓ Knowledge Sharing Sessions:
  Facilitate knowledge-sharing sessions to disseminate insights and best practices
  Encourage cross-functional collaboration in sharing lessons learned
- ✓ Training and Skill Development:
  Identify training needs based on the lessons learned
  Develop training programs to enhance skills related to the improvement initiatives

Note: Customize the template based on the specific improvement initiatives and continuous improvement processes relevant to your organization. Regularly update the log to reflect the dynamic nature of continuous improvement.

Real-life Case Studies

In this chapter, we delve into real-life case studies that illuminate the practical application of sales forecasting principles in various organizational contexts. These case studies provide readers with tangible examples of how companies navigated challenges, implemented strategies, and achieved accurate sales forecasts. By examining these real-world scenarios, readers can gain valuable insights into the nuances of sales forecasting and adapt proven strategies to their own situations.

Case Study 1: Navigating Market Uncertainties

Background: Company X, a mid-sized technology firm, faced heightened market uncertainties due to rapidly evolving technological trends and increasing competition. The company needed to enhance its sales forecasting methods to adapt to the dynamic market landscape.

Challenges:

- ✓ Unpredictable shifts in customer preferences.
- ✓ Emerging technologies impacting product demand.
- ✓ Fluctuating market conditions affecting sales cycles.

Strategies Implemented:

- ✓ Implemented a continuous market analysis framework.
- ✓ Leveraged qualitative insights from customer feedback sessions.
- ✓ Established cross-functional collaboration to integrate market intelligence.

Outcome: Company X successfully navigated market uncertainties by adopting a more agile approach to forecasting. By regularly updating their forecasting models based on market analysis and incorporating qualitative insights, they achieved a more accurate prediction of customer demands, enabling proactive responses to market changes.

Case Study 2: Utilizing Advanced Forecasting Techniques

Background: Company Y, a global consumer goods manufacturer, sought to optimize its forecasting accuracy by incorporating advanced techniques beyond traditional methods. They aimed to leverage machine learning algorithms to uncover complex patterns in their extensive sales data.

Challenges:

- ✓ Large datasets requiring sophisticated analysis.
- ✓ Complex relationships between variables influencing sales.
- ✓ Limited experience with machine learning models.

Strategies Implemented:

- ✓ Invested in machine learning tools and expertise.
- ✓ Collaborated with data scientists to develop custom algorithms.
- ✓ Conducted thorough training for the sales team on interpreting machine learning outputs.

Outcome: By embracing advanced forecasting techniques, Company Y experienced a significant improvement in accuracy. The machine learning models identified subtle patterns in customer behavior, allowing for more precise sales predictions.

This, in turn, streamlined inventory management and optimized resource allocation.

Case Study 3: Overcoming Collaboration Challenges

Background: Company Z, a multinational conglomerate, faced challenges arising from a lack of collaboration between its sales and production departments. Siloed information and misalignment between sales forecasts and production schedules led to inefficiencies and increased costs.

Challenges:

- ✓ Limited communication between sales and production teams.
- ✓ Inaccurate production forecasts impacting inventory levels.
- ✓ Delays in product availability due to misalignment.

Strategies Implemented:

- ✓ Introduced cross-functional workshops to enhance communication.
- ✓ Implemented a shared forecasting platform for sales and production.
- ✓ Established joint KPIs to align sales and production goals.

Outcome: By fostering collaboration between sales and production, Company Z achieved a synchronized forecasting and production process. This resulted in reduced lead times, optimized inventory levels, and improved overall operational efficiency.

Action Plan

Reflect on Similarities:

- ✓ Consider the challenges faced by the companies in the case studies and reflect on any similarities with your organization's situation.

Identify Applicable Strategies:

- ✓ Explore the strategies implemented by these companies and identify those that align with your organization's goals and challenges.

Adaptation for Your Context:

- ✓ Consider how the successful strategies can be adapted to your organization's unique context, taking into account its size, industry, and specific challenges.

Engage in Discussions:

- ✓ Use the case studies as discussion points within your team or organization to encourage dialogue on improving sales forecasting practices.

By engaging with these real-life case studies, readers can gain practical insights and inspiration for implementing effective sales forecasting strategies within their own organizational settings.

Interactive Exercises and Workshops

We will now cover interactive exercises and workshops designed to enhance your engagement and facilitate hands-on application of the sales forecasting concepts discussed in each chapter. These exercises are crafted to encourage active participation, scenario-based discussions, and group activities that empower readers to directly apply the acquired knowledge. The action plan includes the creation of templates to guide readers through these interactive exercises.

Exercise 1: Data Quality Audit Workshop
Objective: To reinforce the importance of data quality in sales forecasting, conduct a Data Quality Audit Workshop.
Workshop Outline:
Introduction (15 minutes):

- ✓ Overview of the significance of data quality in forecasting.
- ✓ Brief explanation of the audit process.

Hands-on Data Quality Audit (30 minutes):

- ✓ Provide a sample dataset with intentional errors.
- ✓ Readers work in groups to identify and document data inconsistencies.

Group Discussion (20 minutes):

- ✓ Each group presents findings and discusses the impact of data quality on forecasting accuracy.

Template Application (15 minutes):

- ✓ Introduce the Data Quality Audit Template for ongoing use.
- ✓ Discuss how regular data quality audits can improve forecasting accuracy.

Exercise 2: Scenario Analysis Simulation

Objective: To develop skills in scenario analysis, conduct a Scenario Analysis Simulation.

Simulation Overview

Introduction (15 minutes):

- ✓ Explanation of scenario analysis and its role in forecasting.
- ✓ Overview of the simulation scenario.

Simulation Activity (45 minutes):

- ✓ Present a hypothetical scenario with market changes.
- ✓ Readers work individually or in groups to adjust forecasts based on the presented scenario.

Group Discussion (20 minutes):

- ✓ Share and discuss the adjustments made by each participant or group.
- ✓ Explore the thought process behind different decisions.

Template Application (15 minutes):

- ✓ Introduce the Scenario Analysis Framework as a tool for ongoing scenario assessments.
- ✓ Discuss the benefits of proactive scenario planning.

Exercise 3: Cross-Functional Collaboration Workshop

Objective: To emphasize the importance of cross-functional collaboration in forecasting, conduct a Cross-Functional Collaboration Workshop.

Workshop Structure

Introduction (20 minutes):

- ✓ Presentation on the impact of collaboration on forecasting accuracy.
- ✓ Overview of collaboration challenges and solutions.

Interactive Discussion (40 minutes):

- ✓ Conduct a scenario-based discussion on a forecasting challenge.
- ✓ Readers engage in cross-functional discussions to propose solutions.

Collaborative Activity (30 minutes):

- ✓ Group activity to design a collaborative forecasting model involving sales, marketing, and production.
- ✓ Encourage participants to identify key touchpoints and information exchange protocols.

Template Application (10 minutes):

- ✓ Introduce the Cross-Functional Collaboration Guide for ongoing collaboration initiatives.
- ✓ Discuss how improved collaboration can enhance forecasting outcomes.

Action Plan

1. Select Relevant Exercises:
   Choose the exercises that align with the specific challenges or focus areas in your organization.
2. Adapt for Your Audience:
   Modify the exercises to suit the knowledge levels and roles of your audience, ensuring relevance and engagement.
3. Facilitate Engaging Discussions:

Act as a facilitator during group discussions, encouraging participants to share insights and learnings.

4. Incorporate Templates:
   Provide participants with the templates introduced in each exercise for ongoing application within their roles.

By incorporating these interactive exercises and workshops, readers can deepen their understanding of sales forecasting concepts and develop practical skills that can be immediately applied in their professional settings.

Conclusion

As we conclude our exploration into the intricacies of sales forecasting, it's essential to recap key concepts and insights gleaned throughout the book. Sales forecasting is both an art and a science, a strategic tool that empowers Sales Managers to make informed decisions and guide their teams toward success.

Recap of Key Concepts and Insights

In this comprehensive guide, we've delved into the fundamental principles of sales forecasting, from the importance of accurate predictions for strategic planning to the diverse methods and techniques available. We've explored the challenges that Sales Managers face, providing actionable strategies to address these hurdles and enhance forecasting accuracy. Key concepts such as data quality, continuous improvement, and cross-functional collaboration have been highlighted as crucial elements in the forecasting process.

Example: Imagine a Sales Manager in a dynamic tech startup. By implementing the insights from this guide, they can refine their forecasting processes, ensuring that they balance historical data with forward-looking indicators, incorporate qualitative factors, foster collaboration among departments, and leverage advanced tools for more accurate predictions.

The Continuous Evolution of Sales Forecasting

Sales forecasting is not a static endeavor; it's a dynamic process that evolves with changes in the business environment, market conditions, and technological advancements. Recognizing the continuous evolution of sales forecasting is key to staying ahead in a rapidly changing landscape.

Example: Consider a Sales Manager in the retail industry. By embracing the continuous evolution of sales forecasting, they can adapt to shifts in consumer behavior, emerging market trends, and advancements in data analytics. This adaptability allows them to refine their forecasting models and stay agile in a competitive market.

Encouragement for Ongoing Learning and Adaptation

In the ever-changing world of sales and business, the pursuit of knowledge and adaptation is paramount. The encouragement for ongoing learning ensures that Sales Managers remain at the forefront of industry trends, emerging technologies, and evolving best practices in sales forecasting.

Action Plan: Create a template for a personal development plan that encourages Sales Managers to set learning goals related to sales forecasting. This plan can include attending industry conferences, enrolling in relevant courses, or engaging in continuous professional development to stay abreast of advancements in forecasting methodologies.

Action Plans and Templates

To support ongoing learning and adaptation, this chapter provides practical action plans and templates. These tools include a template for a personal development plan, a guide for staying informed about industry trends, and a checklist for adapting forecasting processes based on new insights.

Example: A Sales Manager, utilizing the provided templates, can create a personal development plan that outlines specific learning goals, timeframes for achieving them, and the resources needed for continuous improvement in sales forecasting skills.

In conclusion, sales forecasting is not merely a task but a strategic capability that can propel businesses toward success. By embracing the concepts and strategies outlined in this guide, Sales Managers can navigate the complexities of forecasting, make informed decisions, and contribute to the ongoing success of their organizations. As the landscape evolves, the commitment to continuous learning and adaptation will ensure that Sales Managers remain effective leaders in the dynamic world of sales forecasting.

Reflection Prompts:

Recap of Key Concepts:

- ✓ Reflect on the key concepts and insights gained throughout the book.
- ✓ How can these concepts be summarized and shared within your organization?

Continuous Learning Commitment:

- ✓ Consider your commitment to ongoing learning in the field of sales forecasting.
- ✓ What steps can be taken to ensure continuous professional development and adaptation to industry advancements?

Encouragement for Ongoing Application:

- ✓ Reflect on the encouragement for ongoing learning and adaptation provided in the conclusion.
- ✓ How can this encouragement be translated into actionable plans for your professional growth?

Action Plan

- ✓ Set Aside Dedicated Reflection Time:
- ✓ Allocate time at the end of each chapter to engage with the reflection prompts.

Document Insights:

- ✓ Keep a reflection journal or document to capture insights and ideas that emerge during the reflection process.

Initiate Discussions:

- ✓ Use the reflection prompts as discussion starters within your team or organization to foster collective reflection and idea-sharing.

Apply Insights:

- ✓ Act on the insights gained through reflection, adapting and implementing sales forecasting strategies within your unique organizational context.

By consistently engaging with these reflection prompts, readers can deepen their understanding, identify tailored solutions to challenges, and actively contribute to the improvement of sales forecasting practices in their organizations.

Thank you for accompanying us on this journey through the intricate world of sales forecasting. May your forecasting endeavors be both accurate and strategically impactful. Here's to mastering the art and science of sales forecasting and shaping a future of informed, data-driven decision-making.
Happy forecasting!

About the Author 'GERARD ASSEY'

Gerard Assey is a Graduate in Economics, a PGD in Management (HRD) and holds a Doctorate in Leadership. Gerard holds several International Qualifications in Sales, Debt Collection, Training & Teaching, and is a 'Fellow' of the prestigious 'Institute of Sales & Marketing Management'-UK, a Certified NLP Practitioner, a 'Certified Trainer', an 'Accredited Management Teacher-Behavioral Sciences', a 'Certified Competency Facilitator', a 'Certified Management Consultant'- (the International credentials of a professional management consultant, awarded in accordance with global standards of the ICMCI); and a Certification from the University of Michigan in 'Successful Negotiation: Essential Strategies and Skills'

He is also a Member of the 'National Association of Sales Professionals' backed with several years experience in varied industries, both in India and Overseas. He also holds an 'Etiquette Consultant' Certification from the USA (by Sue Fox, Author of Best Seller: 'Business Etiquette for Dummies'. She has trained some of the top celebrities' world over). He was also a recipient of a scholarship for extensive training in Japan on 'Corporate Management for India'.

Gerard Assey is 'Founder & Chief Corporate Trainer' of the Group: '**Citius, Altius, Fortius Unlimited**'- an organization that **celebrated 20 years of Glorious Service** in 2021, focusing on 3 Core Competencies:

People. Performance. Profit; in functional areas of Sales & Marketing, HR & Organizational Development, covering Recruitment, Training & Consultancy!

Having managed organizations with large Sales Forces in India & Overseas, his specialization cover extensive areas of Sales Training (All levels - Presentation, Negotiation, Key/ Strategic Accounts Management & Managerial Skills for all sectors), Bid Proposal/ Capture Planning/ Management Trainings, Retail Sales, Customer Service & Customer Retention Programs, Training for Prevention & Collection of Debt, Self & Personal Development Programs (Time Management, Teamwork & Team Building, Business Etiquette & Personal Grooming, Leadership & Managerial Skills, People Management Skills, Train-the-Trainer etc), including preparation of Custom-designed Business Manuals for Internal (HR, Induction, and Sales etc) & External use (Instruction, User Manuals).

Gerard has successfully conducted over 6050 Trainings & Workshops (as of Jan '24) all across India, Middle East, Africa, Europe & S.E. Asia. Besides public programs conducted regularly, both in India & Overseas, he has some of the top names as clients whom he services from Single Owners to large Public & Government undertakings, covering all sectors, for their in-house needs.

His website: www.CollectionSkills.com is the only one in this part of the world to be featured in the 'Collections & Credit Risk Magazine-USA' under 'Who's Who in Training' and ranks TOP, along with other websites listed below on most search engines.

Gerard is author of 102 books already (Jan 2024)

A few of our business related books:

1. Bite-sized Bits on Commonsense Management
2. Heart to Heart on Life's Principles'
3. How to become a Successful Manager
4. The Sales Professionals' Master Workbook of S.Y.S.T.E.M.S
5. The Professional Business Email Etiquette Handbook & Guide
6. The Professional Business Video-Conferencing Etiquette Handbook & Guide
7. Professional Presentation Skills
8. Exceptional Customer Service
9. Professional Tele-Marketing Skills
10. Professional Debt Collection Skills
11. The G.R.E.A.T. Sales & Service Workbook
12. Sales Training Advantage for Results (*The Ultimate Sales Training Manual to enable you stand out as a S.T.A.R.*)
13. CEO Daily Planner & Organizer
14. The Sales Professionals' Master Daily Planner
15. The Professional Debt Collector's Master Daily Planner
16. My Daily Planner & Organizer
17. MY EMERGENCY INFORMATION RECORD (Family Emergency & Peace of Mind Planner)
18. The Ultimate Therapist & Counselors Planner and Organizer
19. Building an Ethical Workplace
20. Managing Relationships at Work
21. Managing Business Meetings Effectively
22. Effective Delegation Skills
23. Goal Setting for Success
24. B2B Selling by Email
25. Professional Business Etiquette & Grooming
26. Dining Etiquette & Table Manners
27. Effective Networking Skills
28. Grooming, Etiquette & Manners for Teens, Young Adults & Future Leaders
29. Inter-Personal Skills
30. Get Ready, Get Hired!
31. Selling in a Recession
32. Effective Receivables Management in an Economic Downturn!
33. Real Estate & Property Sales Training
34. Credit Sales & Accounts Receivable Management
35. Selling Skills for Real Estate & Property Advisors
36. Take G.R.E.A.T. C.A.R.E!
37. Spa, Salon & Health Club Selling Skills
38. Selling Travel, Holiday & MICE Services
39. Selling Skills for Spa's, Salons & Health Clubs
40. Retailing in Salons & Spas

41. Selling Holiday, Vacation, Tours & Packages
42. The Power of Sales Referrals
43. Selling Luxury
44. Technical Selling Skills
45. Financial Advisors Sales Training
46. Dealing with Burnout at Work Monopolize Your Markets
47. Selling to Affluent Customers
48. Growing up with Grace
49. Financial Selling Skills
50. *The Effective Manager's Guide: Key Skills to Thrive*
51. From Aspiring to Inspiring: A Guide for New Managers on the Rise
52. The Power of Focus
53. Selling with Integrity: Sell Like Jesus The Perfect Role Model!
54. 31 Habits of Champions: Your 31-Day Journey to Greatness
55. Rejecting Grasshopper Talk: From Grasshopper to Giant-Killer-*Defeating Giants Daily!*
56. Navigate the AI-Powered Future of Bid & Proposals: Up-Skill to Stay Relevant with Alternative Career Paths & Opportunities
57. Hiring Sales Winners
58. Present with Impact
59. Success Unlocked: *Breaking Free from Habits that Hold You Back*
60. Complaints to Cheers, Feedback to Gold: Mastering Complaints Management
61. Thriving Together: *Cultivating Diversity, Equity, and Inclusion*
62. Coaching Skills for Sales Managers
63. Soaring to Success in Business & Leadership: Swifter, Higher, Stronger!
64. From Classroom to Podium: A Student's Guide to Powerful Public Speaking & Presentation Skills
65. Developing Self-Discipline
66. The CEO's 31-Day Power Plan: Unlocking Success through Essential Traits
67. Credibility Matters
68. A Winning Attitude
69. Bid & Proposal Management Using AI
70. Sales Forecasting: A Practical & Proven Guide to Strategic Sales Forecasting

Besides regularly contributing to business & trade journals, including international ones such as the 'Creative Training Techniques' and the 'Sales News' of the U.S.A, He is also a member of several prestigious bodies & trade associations, having participated in many Conferences & Workshops in India & Overseas.

Prior to his last assignment of leading & managing a large MNC as head, Gerard had a 3-year stint in the Middle East as a Consultant with a leading British Consultancy Firm.

As the past 'Official Country Representative' for the International Business Award- 'THE STEVIES'-(the business world's own Oscar) for about 4 years- he ensured a few Indian companies that qualify for the same every year!

Gerard can be contacted at:
Email: training@Sales-Training.in,training@CollectionSkills.com
Websites:

www.Sales-Training.in
www.EtiquetteWorks.in
www.CollectionSkills.com
www.RetailSalesTraining.in
www.SalesTrainingIndia.com
www.ManualPreparation.com
www.TrainingWithPuppets.com
www.FirstContactAcademy.com
www.SalesAndMarketingRecruiter.com

Our TRAININGS that can help your team

- ✓ **Sales Effectiveness**: Selling Skills for any Sector: Service/ Logistics/ FMCG Realty/ Insurance & Finance/ Media/ SPA's, Health Clubs & Salons/ Key Account Management, Effective Negotiation Skills/ Bid & Proposal Management Skills/ Retail Sales Training: Any Sector (Auto, Jewelry, Clothing, Luxury etc)
- ✓ **Customer Service Skills**-Complaints Handling & Customer Retention
- ✓ **Debt Prevention & Collection Skills**
- ✓ **Etiquette & Grooming**
- ✓ **Leadership & Managerial Skills**
- ✓ **Self & Personal Development Skills**: Presentation Skills/ Effective Communication Skills/Business Proposal Writing Skills/ Problem Solving & Decision Making Skills/ Empowering Secretaries-The perfect PA! (For Secretaries & PA's)/ Effective Time Management/ Teamwork & Teambuilding/ P.R.I.D.E- **P**ersonal **R**esponsibility **I**n **D**elivering **E**xcellence

www.ingramcontent.com/pod-product-compliance
Lightning Source LLC
LaVergne TN
LVHW010452160826
845677LV00012B/2443

* 9 7 8 8 1 9 6 7 2 0 2 6 1 *